Proven 5-Steps Potty Training In A Weekend

No More Wet Pants, Accidents and Crying!

A STEP BY STEP GUIDE FOR PARENTS WHO ARE TIRED AND FRUSTRATED OVER THE MANY "WET PANTS" ACCIDENTS AND WANT TO ACCELERATE THE POTTY TRAINING PROCESS TO JUST 1 WEEKEND

PATRICK BRADLEY

You agree to accept all risks of using the information presented inside this book.

You agree that by continuing to read this book, where appropriate and/or necessary, you shall consult a professional (including but not limited to your doctor, attorney, or financial advisor or such other advisor as needed) before using any of the suggested remedies, techniques, or information in this book.

TABLE OF CONTENTS

Introduction 1

Chapter 1...3

  Potty training – what you must know 3

Chapter 2...13

  5 steps potty training that works 13

Chapter 3...21

  Additional tips to ensure your success 21

Chapter 4...29

  How to create a potty training plan for your child?................29

Chapter 5...35

  Summary of key action plans 35

Chapter 6...39

  Making success sweeter 39

Conclusion 43

INTRODUCTION

Most children still wet their pants for a year or more after learning, so be patient if you are going through a similar process. Do not worry!

Most children learn to go to the toilet between 2 and 4 years and learn to do it at night at the age of eight. However, the potty training that we propose in this eBook can be applied to children from 18 months to 3 years old.

Potty training can be a long and frustrating process. If you try to start training before your child is ready, you cannot force him to learn.

In this eBook, you will know the secret to success. You will find strategies, steps, techniques, and tips that will be useful for you to succeed in your work.

CHAPTER 1

Potty training – what you must know

Potty training occurs very naturally in children. If you deploy the right techniques, children can learn faster than you think.

Why potty training is essential

Using potty is an important skill in the daily life of your child. Having changed about two thousand diapers a year (6 a day), you're probably looking forward to your little one starting to use potty alone. More important point is that the potty training promotes the overall development of your child.

Promotes self-image and confidence

Potty training affirms your child that he/she is no longer a baby and reaffirms his/her gender and control over his/her life. Learning to use the potty promotes self-image and self-confidence which help your child to achieve more milestones in the future.

Save money

If you buy disposable diapers, you will save a lot of money with potty training. Those Disposable diapers could be replaced with enrichment materials which would promote your child's mental growth. If you use cloth diapers, the hassle of changing and washing the diapers goes away when your child knows how to use the potty.

Attend enriching school activities

Many schools or extracurricular activities require that children can use the toilet alone. If you trained your child before the age of three, he might be able to enroll in the extracurricular activities.

When is a good time to start?

It typically happens between 18 months and 3 years across both genders, although there are exceptions.

Signs that a child is ready to begin training do not vary but could occur at different ages.

When, and how to start?

1-Hold periods of two hours or more without wetting the diaper

One of the first indicators is the time when the child no longer wet the diaper regularly. That means it can stay dry between two and three hours. When that happens, it means that your child has reached an initial control of the muscles and possessed the ability to retain or endure.

2-Time to make him discover his powers

It is very natural that child has not even realized that he already has this capacity, which is why the next step is to make him understand that he can control the need to use the potty. The exercise will do the rest, and this is the training period for them to learn the steps to follow.

3-Adaptations accessible in the family toilet

It is a good idea to buy an attractive potty that your child likes. If you can buy it with him/her while you talk about the purpose of having his/her own space. It is easy for him/her to access it, and the child will feel happy and excited. Place the potty in an accessible place, and try to leave the door open so that it is easy to reach without major obstacles.

4-Award when the mission has been completed

Parties, applause and a box of stickers are always motivating. There are many ways to motivate and affirm your child in this task. You can give him a sticker as a reward, and even a chewable gummy multi-vitamin or something special that he enjoys. It is important that the child also learns that after occupying his potty, you will help him empty it into the toilet and keep it clean.

5-Understanding the importance of hygiene since he is small

Little by little he/she will learn to use toilet paper. While there could be many accidents, it is important to reinforce your child that he/she can do better the next time. Remember to instruct the good habits of washing his hands with soap and water after he goes to the bathroom.

No more pulling of hairs - it's all about the right technique!

Handle accidents positively. Accidents are common, understandable, and may happen for few months or years even after the child has been trained. You have to adopt a positive attitude, understand the root causes of these accidents and never blame to shame the child.

Most children give clues that they need the potty. Then, sometimes you have to run, and explain to them again and again what you are doing and expect from them. Do not mistreat your child and always teach with love. Recognize this is not a skill that children could learn within a single day.

What you should do in an "accident":

- Relax, avoid getting angry, be consistent and try to make learning casual and through games.

- Choose a word to describe he wants to urinate or defecate that he can use whenever he wants the potty for pee or poop. Keep in mind that he will use these words everywhere, so it is important these keywords do not embarrass him/her.

- Speak to him/her like an adult and explain to him/her the purpose of using a toilet during teachable moments (e.g. when your child walks past a toilet in the shopping).

- Avoid using offensive words such as dirty, bad, and stinky as they will embarrass him/her and even detest the potty.

- During diaper change something that you enjoy and tell him he can get close to you and let you know when he feels wet or dirty.

- Remember that a balanced diet will help the stools to become regular and the process more comfortable and painless.

- Remember to remove any substance that may be dangerous from the toilet or potty.

Golden rules of potty training: Boys vs. girls

Children learn by imitating adults, so the most natural way for them to learn to use the potty is to watch you do it at the toilet.

If he is a boy

It is easier to start peeing, and later on, Dad or an older brother will teach him to pee standing. Surely he will not take long to imitate him.

When you are showing your child how to use the potty, it is good for you to explain what you are doing, show him what you have "produced", and show him that in the end you clean, you dress, you pull the chain and you wash your hands.

Although you will have to help him get off, put on his clothes and clean himself for some time, seeing you or his brother doing it will help him understand the process.

If she is a girl

If you have a girl, make sure she wipes from front to back, especially after pooping, to reduce the risk of urinary tract infections.

If there is a little sister who already knows how to use the potty, she can also give a demonstration to the little one. Children pay close attention when "teachers" are about the same age as them.

Useful tools to accelerate potty training

When training your child for the potty, there are some things you can do to make that process more comfortable for both of you.

1-Children's bath seats

The toilets scare many young children. If your child does not want to know anything about the potty, give him a bath chair and help him to feel more comfortable, after that he will consider it as his own.

What if he is afraid of the car seat?

If this is the case with your baby, all you need is a cushioned seat with a narrow opening and handles, which is placed in the toilet to make him more comfortable. Also, your child will feel completely safe with this seat.

Even some seats have water filled cushions or musical sound when your child uses them. Others have steps to make it easier for him to reach the toilet and later become a tool that encourages him to brush his teeth and wash his hands.

Age range

You will want to buy a bath chair when your child is around 18 months of age. It is suggested that you should put that seat in the toilet so that he can become more acquainted with it a great deal before he is prepared to use it.

If he is a boy

If you have a boy, look for a chamber pot without the seat going up and down, or bring one that can be removed.

Although this type of seat helps to prevent the little boy from spilling some water out of the potty, they have the disadvantage that child often hits or scratches the penis when sitting and getting up, which can take away the desire to use the potty.

2- Funny underwear

This idea is very simple but often effective. If each time they have to do pee or poop and see, and remember, that they are wearing underpants or panties with drawings of their favorite characters, this will seem fun and they will associate positive feelings to that moment. In this way, it may even happen that, as soon as they feel like urinating or defecating, these characters come to mind and go to the potty to "be with them".

3. Play with play-dough and water

Use some games that help the child in the purpose of leaving the diaper. We advise, on the one hand, games with water.

Take the liquid from one container to another, with glasses, funnels and other equipment. In this way, the child plays with the idea of when to stop and prevent the passage of water and "reinforces the idea of continence.

A child plays a lot with play-dough, in order to satisfy his curiosity towards his own excrement. Familiarizing himself with the poop is another step in the process of leaving diapers, and this game is a good resource to help that end.

4-Stories

Stories have the ability to convey to children messages that are difficult to convey in another way. The protagonists of these stories often face various issues related to their physiological needs, such as using the potty for the first time or getting up at night to do so. The drawings in the books, in addition, help the child identify with such situations.

5-Songs

Like the stories, the songs are also very funny and children like them a lot. One of the best songs known as the 'Song of the pee and the poop'.

There is a Japanese drawing that shows a little boy who is learning to do pee and poop in the toilet. The lyrics of the song are in Japanese and do not include subtitles, but, as it is very animated, it can also be an incentive for the little ones.

A success story of a parent that succeeded in potty training

The first year of my baby's life was incredible, as I marveled at all the developmental milestones that he reaches. It was very beautiful to see my little one as he learns to lift his head, crawl and explore the world around him.

However, something that I had in mind, as he was growing up was the right time to start the potty training. I did not know what to do; I just had to spend a lot of many to buy thousands of diapers a year. Between 12 and 18 months of age, there is very little control.

Until one day I decided not to buy more diapers and I started the potty training. It was amazing! That training presented by me was very satisfactory, and the result I got for just one week in two different approaches. The first was the approach of waiting for the child to be ready, which usually takes much longer than early potty training. The second was to teach my son when I think he is prepared to the point of view of development. I decided to try the second one. There are numerous advantages in this, including an easier and faster training process.

It was a good time for my son to learn and practice habits that allow him to stay healthy, clean and comfortable. That helped me show him how to clean himself to avoid getting infections or staining his clothes by teaching him to wash his hands when he finished.

When you realize that the best method is to prepare your child for the potty training and do it following the necessary steps; this makes your heart happy.

CHAPTER 2

5 steps potty training that works

The training to leave the diapers covers a series of individual skills. You have to be able to interpret the signals you child emits; that means, to undress, to have control of the bladder and the intestines and to wash the hands. That's why in this chapter, we're going to see 5 steps potty training. Now, the question is following;

How to pick the "right" weekend

Before entering on those steps, you have to choose a time when you can spend long periods with your child at home, especially on the weekend, so that he feels comfortable and safe with his environment and always have you to encourage and support him.

That is why it is important to start the potty training when you can devote time and energy to help your child learn this new skill.

Remember, if you work on the weekend and you have time during the week, you can choose 2-3 days during the week. Yes! Choosing the right time to train your child how to use the potty can greatly determine your chances of success.

5 steps potty training

Step #1: Preparation

First, before starting, motivate him/her with words such as: "You can do it." "You are a champion, you will win" and "I know you can".

Avoid teaching him if he has recently gone through a period of change, for example, if his brother or sister was born, if he has moved from home or if he has started to go to another daycare center, because those changes could be stressful for a child and teaching him to use the potty will only stress it more.

Get a potty

Many children feel more secure starting with one that rests on the floor instead of leaning on the toilet. It is less frightening and gives them the security and balance they need to be able to support their feet on the floor.

Place the potty in a convenient place and let your child spend most of the time. It is not necessary to have it in the bathroom. You can keep it in a corner in the game room. Easy access is important at the beginning.

Allow your child to explore and become familiar with the potty. Let him feel that he is special and that it is for him.

Step #2: Establish a schedule

1. A fixed schedule can help to make the potty training time in a routine which will help the child adapt to his new responsibility and help him remember to go on his own. Have your child sit at least 15 minutes a day in the potty 2 to 3 times a day. If he uses it, excellent, but if not, do not worry. It is only necessary for the child to get used to it.

2. If he gets impatient to go out, give him a book or a toy to play with so he does not think the potty is a punishment.

3. Never force him to sit in the potty if he does not want to, but you will only make him resist more, which can affect the entire training process.

4. To encourage your child to go to use the potty, try to choose times of the day when he is most likely to need a bath, for example, first thing in the morning, after eating and before bedtime.

5. Make time in the potty part of his routine before going to sleep: have him put on his pajamas, wash his face, brush his teeth and sit in his potty. Soon he will remember doing it alone.

Date

AM	7:00	8:00	9:00	10:00	11:00	12:00
PM	1:00	2:00	3:00	4:00	5:00	6:00

PM	7:00	8:00	9:00	10:00	11:00	12:00

Step #3: Learning time

1. Have your child practice sitting in the potty, dressed allowing him to get up whenever he wants. Your goal makes him being comfortable with the new object.

2. Congratulate your child for every advance he/she demonstrates, including every step he takes as small as he is and even if he has not completed it. Keep optimism. Remember that this is his achievement and not yours.

You can use the words of joy to motivate him, such as: "What a nice surprise you gave me, I love it". "I congratulate you for what you have done, it makes me very happy". "I see that you are improving every day."

1. Once he feels comfortable sitting in the dress pot, you can allow him to practice without clothes. This will help him become familiar with the concept of undressing before going to the toilet; it will also allow him/her to feel the seat on his skin.

2. After a few days, when your child has gone through the diaper, throw that in the potty so he can see where he/she should go. Explain that this is where urine and poop should be.

3. Observe the indications of your child's need to urinate or poop. Some children will tell you with words. Others will growl, make gestures and put themselves in a particular position. When this happens, ask if he wants to go to the toilet.

4. Alternatively, allow him to walk around the house for a few days without pants. Remind him every hour he/she tries to use the potty. This will help him/her interpret the signals his body sends him.

5. Share what you are doing with other family members and people who are parts of the child's life, such as babysitters or close friends. In this way, your child will perceive expectations and consistent support which will facilitate the transition.

6. You can also give more fluids with his food if you want, as this will help speed up his digestive system. Never let your child get dirty diapers, either with urine or poop, in an attempt to "train" him. That will only make the situation worse.

Hours of liquid consumptio n	Pee time	Differenc e	Hours of food consumptio n	Poop time	Differenc e

	Averag e			**Averag e**	

Step #4: Reinforcement

1. Congratulate your child at each stage of learning. It's a good idea to congratulate him/her when he/she tells you he wants to use the potty, even if you just asked him/her the question.

2. Expect him to make mistakes, especially at the beginning. If your child is reluctant to do something new, it's probably because he is not ready yet. Just wait and try again in a couple of days or even weeks.

3. Once your child has been successful for a few days, start with the transition to wearing underwear. Remember that your child can feel more comfortable not only wearing diapers but also using

training pants. Also, it may be that your child likes to wear underwear. Whatever your child's reaction is, try to let his response to help you in the process.

4. Remember that some young children have measured the noise or toilet actions. If he is afraid, do not force him to let the water run; do it when he leaves the toilet. Fear usually goes away with the passing of months. But if he does it right, encourage him with motivational words.

You can use the words of satisfaction and confidence, as for example: "I like it that way, you did it very well". "I already know that you would do well." "I am very proud of you". "I know you're good and you can do it"...

Step #5: Night training

1. In the beginning, let your child wear diapers to sleep and tell him that if he wakes up and wants to go to the toilet, he can call you. You can also leave his potty handy if he wants to try it alone.

2. When your little one spends five nights in a row without getting wet or pooping, it will be time to start the evening instruction. Use a plastic or waterproof fabric between the sheet and the mattress and put it without diapers. If you think he/she is not learning, go back to the diapers and try after a few months.

3. Be consistent with preparation, learning, and reinforcement. You will be surprised at how quickly he will get rid of diapers.

Additional tips for potty training

*   Children feel more stable and comfortable in the toilet if their feet are flat. Move a bench closer so that your child can rest his feet if

he is using a regular size cup. The small seats that are placed on the toilet also help to make them feel more secure.

- Pay attention to the toilet seat when you are outside with them.

- Change the clean clothes in case your child has an accident in public.

- Never leave your child unsupervised. If your child wants privacy, wait outside the door.

- Teach good hygiene, such as washing his hands thoroughly and cleaning himself after going to the toilet. Check after your child has been swept in case he has not been done well.

- Accidents at night are common up to five years, so don't blame or humiliate your child.

- Medical problems including frequent constipation can make it difficult to teach your child to use the toilet. If your child is 4 ½ to 5 years old and is unable to get used to using the toilet, or if you have any concerns you might see a physical problem or you are unsure if a medical condition will affect your child's ability to be able to use the toilet, talk to your child's pediatrician.

CHAPTER 3

Additional tips to ensure your success

For the boys

Tip #1: Get something to point to

Small cheerios or other things that float are a good option to have your child urinates inside the potty. Just tell him to hold his private part and point to the designated element. Alternatively, place a sticker on the bottom of his potty training chair.

Tip #2: Teach him to feel comfortable holding his penis

Although we always encourage children not to play with it in public, your child should feel comfortable holding back and directing his flow to where he should go. This is a great job that should be taught by an older brother, father or uncle.

Tip #3: Choose a pot that has a "Lip"

Some children's pots have a small hump or cup in the front, which is designed to catch the flow of your child if he shoots on the edge of the seat while learning to go to the toilet.

1. The boys and girls are different, especially because the children will eventually need to learn to stand and pee.

2. Allow your child to learn the potty training in a child-specific way. That will help prevent future struggles.

There are some of the tips you should use while teaching your child to use the toilet. Include giving him something to aim for, teaching him to hold his private parts and using a potty that has a cup or tab to catch the lost urine while he is sitting to do poop.

For the girls

In girls, urinary tract infections, although not very common, seem to occur more frequently during the potty training period.

If you notice that your daughter needs to urinate frequently, has pain when urinating, begins to pee on after learning to use the potty, has abdominal pain, or has sudden and urgent urge to urinate, call the doctor, as these may be the symptoms of an infection.

What if she wants to pee standing?

If your daughter has seen her father, brother or a child at the daycare stand peeing, she may want to try.

It's okay if you let her do so, except you'll have to clean her, but she will probably soon realize that she does not have the "equipment" for that method to work and leave it without you having to argue.

Although, if you insist, let her watch you peeing and explain that the mothers and girls sit down to urinate.

When to move from potty to loo?

Replacing the potty with the toilet is a step that the child should perform in a relaxed manner, and if you turn the use of the toilet in an obligation, she ends up rejecting it sharply.

How to make this change easier for you?

1-Use the reducer

It attaches to the toilet seat and, as the name suggests, reduces its size. It is convenient that it is always placed; so, as your child progresses in his new learning, he can start using the cup independently, without having to warn each time he needs to pee (for a while you will have to remove it when you go to the bathroom and put it back.)

2-You need the stair

It is a small stool that allows the child two things: reach the required height to sit easily and has his feet supported while he is using the toilet, which provides security.

The stair also helps constipated children to poop, because leaning on, he can make more strength. Another advantage of this accessory is that it can be used as an elevator to reach the tap and soap and wash his hands more comfortably.

3-The wipes

A little further on, in order to your child can clean his bum by himself, and do it well, buy him a box of specific wipes for this use, which can be flushed down the toilet without risk of clogging.

What if he does not want to leave the potty?

Many children are reluctant to use the toilet because it is a change in their comfortable routines.

In no case, should the child be forced to use the toilet whenever he does not want to? Yes! Accompany him for a few days, once he decides to use it. Nor do you have to radically replace the potty with the toilet.

You can combine both until the child decides to say goodbye to his potty forever.

The method of posters

Starting to use the toilet is not enough to be an older child. Also, he has to clean himself, pull the chain (unless the noise scares him), lower the lid and then wash his hands.

So that your child does not forget any of these tasks you can stick in the bathroom a sequence of posters that remind him what he has to do. The idea will enchant him and help him to be more autonomous.

Is it possible to teach even if your child has no communication skills or in daycare?

Not having communication skills does not influence anything to get it or not, although it is possible that you find more difficulties in communication to explain certain things. From here we recommend that you use all the resources at your fingertips: signs, drawings, expressiveness ... Surely little by little you will get better. They are also fit if your child has autism.

1. Know the parts of the body. Knowing how to place them, knowing its name and/or sign is a great idea to start with the process of leaving the diaper.

2. Drawings in the bathroom. A good idea may be to put some drawings in the bathroom explaining the steps: lower your pants, clean with paper, pull the chain; a very visual way for him to understand it and have fun watching it. Surely there are many drawings on the Internet.

3. The key signs. Pee, poop, pants, clean, toilet paper, toothbrush, comb, towel, gel. Knowing these signs related to hygiene and bath will serve you well.

4. Avoid liquids at night. When you start to remove the diaper at night, it is best not to drink a lot of liquid before going to sleep.

What are other useful strategies especially for children with autism?

- Make the bathroom a positive place (with music, dim lighting, pleasant aromas, etc.);

- Reduce the fear of sitting on the toilet, placing a footrest for stabilization;

- Plan beforehand what clothes the child is going to wear as well as to make it easier to take off their clothes;

- Make a basket of your child's favorite games that will only be allowed to play with while sitting on the toilet;

- Use a minute hand to increase the amount of time you sit on the toilet;

- Create a blackboard that details each step ('first and then ...', called "first-then" (for example, "First sit down, then make bubbles");

- Use stories and social stories that describe each step of the process through a simple format;

- Create a picture card to communicate the need to use the bathroom, if your child is non-verbal.

Potential regression scenarios and what you can do about it

It is advisable not to scold him, or create a dramatic situation out of it.

Children who refuse to stand

Some young children will refuse to urinate standing up since they initially sat in it. Instead of doing a drama, let your child do what he wants until he is ready to stand up. Eventually, he will learn.

Young children should have a strong, arched stream; otherwise, they need an evaluation. If a drip suddenly occurs, it could be an indicator of infection.

Children who go into hiding

In this situation, providing comfort and guidance is much better than scolding. If you find poop or a puddle behind the chair or curtain, try to avoid direct pronouns and direct language ("" Did you poop behind the curtain? ""). Your face will show that you are disappointed. Your words should only provide instructions to handle the problem in a better way.

Infections

Many signs have to do with urinary tract infection. These signs may be: Pain or burning when urinating, cloudy or smelly urine, blood or pus in his urine, pressure or cramping in the abdomen. Consult your child's doctor if the child has any of these symptoms.

Stress

Your child may feel quite stressed and cry in the training process; such feelings prevent him from doing pee and poop; something that can cause constipation. Below, we give you the instructions to avoid those problems:

1. Put the diaper training on hold for a while. Go back and take it back in one to three months, and ask your child if he is ready to try it at that moment. Retention is a power game in which the child wins. So do not participate in combat.

2. If keeping the poop is the cause of constipation, it is easy to find treatment for that. What you have to do is use a lot of fiber and fruit in your child's diet. Also, you can use soft softeners or laxatives.

If the problem is not resolved within a week, consult the doctor.

What if your child dislikes the potty?

Tell your child that you understand his fear, be patient and help him like this:

A trick for many is to put the diaper for this moment, but each time a little lower so they learn the process of "letting go". Finally, there will be hardly any difference between resorting to the diaper and doing it in the potty. And from the potty will give way to the toilet with a reducer installed on the lid.

1. Make the moment as pleasant as possible.

2. Explain the bodily functions through a book so that he understands that it is something natural.

3. A doll with a toy pot allows him to recreate his situation and "elaborate" it by playing.

4. Playing with playdough, mud, sand or finger paint is therapeutic. These materials help him to assimilate fears unconsciously.

5. Celebrate his successes and ignore his accidents. The less pressure, the easier the learning will be.

6. All children, sooner or later, end up overcoming this problem.

7. You should not make him sit in the potty for prolonged periods

8. Take him to the pediatrician. He will prescribe a diet rich in fiber and possibly, at first, a laxative.

9. Sit him in the potty 5-10 minutes after each meal so that the gastro-colic reflex, bowel contractions, is activated.

10. Hang a folio in the kitchen and draw a smiling sun on it every time he does his belly. When you add three soles, give him a little gift.

CHAPTER 4

How to create a potty training plan for your child?

It is possible for you to help your child to learn the use of the potty and the toilet more ahead. A lot of people can help, such as; family members, teachers, assistants, and the center's staff. All the people who deal with your child should use the same vocabulary and follow the same routine. This has been a great success.

Having a written teaching plan can help your child. If the plan is in writing, everyone can use the same vocabulary and follow the same routine. A teaching plan could include these details:

Goals

✓ Communicate your goals to your child's assistant. Explain to the assistant exactly what you are trying to achieve during a certain period. For example, "My goal is for Jameson to go the potty 15 minutes after the supper and sit in the latrine for 5 seconds."

Routine

✓ How often? Include the frequency or time of his potty visits. For example, "each hour, on the hour" or "15 minutes subsequent to drinking/eating something."

✓ For how long? Be sure to specify how long your child can sit down - it may be only 5 seconds in the beginning.

Vocabulary

✓ **Words**: Use words that your child understands. For example, are there "code" words that you usually use to mean "urinate"? What words do you use to tell your child to go to the potty or toilet?

Places

- ✓ **Place**: Where does your child go to the potty or toilet?
- ✓ **Details**: Think of the lights. Are they strong or light? How do the lights affect your child? What kind of noises are there in the toilet (e.g., a fan)? What type of toilet paper is used? Should the door be open or closed?
- ✓ **People**: Who accompanies your child to the potty? Does that person come in with your son, or does he just stay close?

Resources

- ✓ What resources are you using? Do you use a visual program? Does your child like music or read a book?

Rewards

- ✓ What are the activities for which you give a reward to your child? Why do not you give it?
- ✓ How do you reward your son when he does well what he should do well? What happens if your child does not receive a reward?

Frequently asked questions

Question #1:

How do I know if it's a false alarm?

Answer:

Observe the behavior of the child. When children really want to go to the toilet, you will see them dancing, moving and, sometimes, touching their genitals. Or, if they feel like pooping, they will squat.

Question #2:

Should I use a potty or sit the child directly on the toilet?

Answer:

It is recommended to use a potty because the little one will feel more comfortable when feeling that the feet touch the floor. If he chooses the toilet, place a small stool that is sturdy and suitable for climbing, but makes sure your child can also support the feet.

Question #3:

My son wants to stand when he goes to the toilet. Should I let him do it from the beginning?

Answer:

If he wants to, leave him. It is possible for a young child to want to copy his father or older brother who could simplify learning to go to the toilet. Just standing requires more coordination between the eyes and the hands.

Question #4:

Why my child can pee in the potty without problems but not poop?

Answer:

Evacuation requires more effort and often generates more complications, such as constipation, or traumatic experiences, such as pain. That can make it harder for the child to poop, even when he has urgency.

Question #5:

Why does it seem that teaching girls to go to the toilet is easier than the boys?

Answer:

There is no clear reason, but a lot of speculation. Perhaps there are differences in development: as with so many other important events. Boys will, in general, develop somewhat later than girls. This can also be related to hygiene and girls tend to be more interested in being cleaner and drier than boys.

Question #6:

Our son uses the toilet at school but refuses to do it at home. What should we do?

Answer:

For many children, it can be difficult to do something at home that they have learned to do at school. It may be helpful for your child to use different restrooms at school. Use the same words and ideas that their teachers use at school. It may help to start with simple steps at home. At first, just walk to the toilet with your child. Go adding steps to the process until he gets to use the toilet at home. Practice going to a different toilet. Use the toilet in stores, and in other people's houses.

Question #7:

We thought we had a good teaching plan for our daughter, but it is not working. What should we do now?

Answer:

You can choose a variety of steps.

1-Make sure there are no medical reasons. Talk to your daughter's doctor to see if she is constipated, or ask her for ideas about a diet change.

2-*Check your daughter's toilet schedule to make sure you are taking her to the potty when she is likely to urinate or evacuate.*

3-*Consider changing your reward. When necessary, change the type of reward you give your child every 3 months. It would also be good to review it, as an excellent behavior modification strategy it is, frequently.*

Question #8:

I was trying to teach my son to use the potty all weekend, but we have not advanced anywhere. How long is the process supposed to take?

Answer:

Some children take a lot of time learning how to use the potty. It is better to remain relaxed and have patience. There is no deadline to learn. The process of teaching your child to use the potty should form only a small part of his life. You can stop and try again when you feel more active, and your child seems ready. Remember that it can be difficult to learn to go to the potty alone. Practice it at a time that is convenient for you and your family. In this way, you will have the necessary energy to teach this important long-term skill.

Question #9:

Is it normal for children to have many accidents during their potty training?

Answer:

Sometimes accidents continue for months after the learning process to use the toilet has already been completed - even if the child is 3 or 4 years old. However, very frequent accidents in children of three years can be a sign of a physical problem or a problem of development. The best thing to do is talk to the child's pediatrician.

CHAPTER 5

Summary of key action plans

Finally, we come to the last chapter of our eBook. We have learned a lot about potty training.

In the first chapter, we have seen why potty training is essential. Going to the toilet is an important skill in daily life. Families need to establish a clear routine to go to the toilet. This will help the child succeed in school and in social situations.

It is important that families begin potty training at the right time for the child, typically between 18 months and 3 years of age. Potty training requires a family commitment; all the members must collaborate so that the process is successful.

The toilet can be an intimidating place with many sounds, sensations, and smells. We have seen some strategies to establish a good routine for the use of potty include making the place accessible and palatable:

- Use urinals, toilet seats or footrests.

- Talk with the child about the bathroom and about how the toilet works to keep it from freaking out.

- Place the objects that will be needed, such as toilet paper, in an accessible place. And have a sturdy stool nearby that helps the child arrive in case he uses the toilet.

- Allow the child to do an activity while in the potty, such as reading his favorite book.

In the second chapter, we talked about the 5 steps to that training:

- How to pick the "right" weekend

- Detailed and proven 5 steps training technique

- Motivational words to use for each phase

- Additional tips for potty training

Those 5 steps summarize the learning and the importance of motivating the child for that training. Some children may also need help cleaning themselves after going to the toilet. Washing his hands is important, and children should be able to access the sink using a sturdy stool. It is recommended to place the soap and towels in an accessible place.

Accidents are frequent and are part of the learning process of the use of the toilet. Reward the children for their responsibility and participation by praising them for their "big boy" or "big girl" underwear, and congratulating them for having succeeded in keeping their bed and their clothes dry.

If a child cannot remember all the steps in the training process, sticking a series of drawings next to the toilet with each step can help. Children need practice and going to the toilet is an activity that requires a lot of patience. Do not blame or humiliate the child.

We also have been considered an important aspect in our eBook on potty training in the third chapter. That has to do with key consideration to ensure your success. Although the child learns to recognize the clues that his body gives to know when he should go to the toilet, you can also help by encouraging routines:

- Teach him to go to the bathroom when he wakes up, before and after a nap, before meals, before going to bed and leaving the house for an activity.

- When to move from potty to loo

- Potential regression scenarios and what you can do about it, etc.

Remember, a child must be prepared physically and mentally to learn how to use the toilet. Babies cannot control their muscles to keep the bladder and rectum closed until they reach 18 months. Maybe if he feels it before this age, your baby will urinate, but he will not be able to control when he does not have the urge to urinate.

CHAPTER 6

Making success sweeter

Helping your child to leave the diapers is not something simple. Therefore, you have to make that process easy and friendly to him. Below, we are going to give you some fun things you can do with your child to get success in the process.

Fun things you can do now that your child is potty trained

1-Make a Potty Party

You can make a special party at that moment. But what you can do is invite other children so that your child is not the only one who is training to go to the toilet. Everything depends on you if you want to do something big or small. The idea is that your child is not alone. That will reinforce him positively when he sees all his friends are peeing and pooping in the potty or toilet.

Also, if you cannot make a party, it can be lunch. It could be another family that has children of his age. So you will see how that will be perfect. Allow your child to announce to friends, family members (those who will excite, cooperate and understand the process) that he is training to go to the potty or toilet.

2-The rain cane

If he likes to go out and take the bathe in the rain, you can make that moment more fun even when it's raining. Among those that you can do in the process, it is the rain stick that is among the favorite fun games. First, because it is very simple and second because it will powerfully surprise your child while sitting in the potty.

Use the cardboard tube of the baking paper or the aluminum foil when it is finished. Close one end, seal with cellophane tape to prevent leakage. Then introduce open beans or dry pasta through the open end, you can also put small stones. When you have added a small amount, even close the other end of the tube, it will help to prevent leakage.

When you turn to one end and the other to the tube, your little one will think that it is the sound of the rain. This will encourage him to sit in the potty.

3-Help him create his own music

Fill the water bottles with rice or beans to make a maraca. Make him hit a bowl of oatmeal used as a drum. Sing silly songs while you move in front of him and while he is sitting on the potty. Soon, you will see that he will pee or poop in the potty.

4-Use some fun apps

There are many fun applications that through animated stories teach children to leave the diaper. Some of them are:

Potty Time, Pull-ups (Big Kids), Potty Show, Potty Baby, Elmo Potty Time, I have to go, Going Potty with (Winkidos), The new Potty, and so on.

CONCLUSION

Finally, you must know that young children love to be like their dad or older brother and learn a lot by imitating the people around them, so seeing another man sitting or getting up from the toilet is a great way to show him how it's done. It's also a very good way to help him gain the confidence to try it for himself. Do not worry if there are no suitable male models when he is ready to begin training, just show him how to sit, then he can learn to get up.

For the girl, make sure she learns to always clean from front to back. This will help prevent bacteria in the rectum from coming into contact with the sensitive skin of the vulva and vagina, preventing it from contracting an infection. When you explain the parts of her body, it is important to be anatomically correct.

Potty training is a big change for children, and it is not a race, accidents happen, and it is important to try to be positive throughout the process. If your child rejects the potty, do not try to push him, he will appreciate it when he is ready.

-- *Patrick Wadley*

Made in the USA
Middletown, DE
12 June 2019